foundations

SMALL GROUP STUDY

tauGHt by tom HoLLaDay anD kay waRReN

CREATION

ZONDERVAN®

SADDLEBACK CHURCH

ZONDERVAN.com/
AUTHORTRACKER
follow your favorite authors

ZONDERVAN®

Foundations: *Creation Study Guide*
Copyright © 2003, 2004, 2008 by Tom Holladay and Kay Warren

Requests for information should be addressed to:
Zondervan, *Grand Rapids, Michigan 49530*

ISBN 978-0-310-27678-4

08 09 10 11 12 13 14 15 16 17 18 • 23 22 21 20 19 18 17 16 15 14 13 12 11 10 9 8 7 6 5 4 3 2 1

foundations TABLE OF CONTENTS

FOREWORD

What *Foundations* Will Do for You

I once built a log cabin in the Sierra Mountains of northern California. After ten backbreaking weeks of clearing forest land, all I had to show for my effort was a leveled and squared concrete foundation. I was discouraged, but my father, who built over a hundred church buildings in his lifetime, said, "Cheer up, son! Once you've laid the foundation, the most important work is behind you." I've since learned that this is a principle for all of life: you can never build *anything* larger than the foundation can handle.

The foundation of any building determines both its size and strength, and the same is true of our lives. A life built on a false or faulty foundation will never reach the height that God intends for it to reach. If you skimp on your foundation, you limit your life.

That's why this material is so vitally important. *Foundations* is the biblical basis of a purpose-driven life. You must understand these life-changing truths to enjoy God's purposes for you. This curriculum has been taught, tested, and refined over ten years with thousands of people at Saddleback Church. I've often said that *Foundations* is the most important class in our church.

Why You Need a Biblical Foundation for Life

- *It's the source of personal growth and stability.* So many of the problems in our lives are caused by faulty thinking. That's why Jesus said the truth will set us free and why Colossians 2:7a (CEV) says, *"Plant your roots in Christ and let him be the foundation for your life."*

- *It's the underpinning of a healthy family.* Proverbs 24:3 (TEV) says, *"Homes are built on the foundation of wisdom and understanding."* In a world that is constantly changing, strong families are based on God's unchanging truth.

- **It's the starting point of leadership.** You can never lead people farther than you've gone yourself. Proverbs 16:12b (MSG) says, *"Sound leadership has a moral foundation."*

- **It's the basis for your eternal reward in heaven.** Paul said, *"Whatever we build on that foundation will be tested by fire on the day of judgment . . . We will be rewarded if our building is left standing"* (1 Corinthians 3:12, 14 CEV).

- **God's truth is the only foundation that will last.** The Bible tells us that *"the sound, wholesome teachings of the Lord Jesus Christ . . . are the foundation for a godly life"* (1 Timothy 6:3 NLT), and that *"God's truth stands firm like a foundation stone . . . "* (2 Timothy 2:19 NLT).

Jesus concluded his Sermon on the Mount with a story illustrating this important truth. Two houses were built on different foundations. The house built on sand was destroyed when rain, floods, and wind swept it away. But the house built on the foundation of solid rock remained firm. He concluded, *"Therefore everyone who hears these words of mine and puts them into practice is like a wise man who built his house on the rock"* (Matthew 7:24 NIV). *The Message* paraphrase of this verse shows how important this is: *"These words I speak to you are not incidental additions to your life . . . They are foundational words, words to build a life on."*

I cannot recommend this curriculum more highly to you. It has changed our church, our staff, and thousands of lives. For too long, too many have thought of theology as something that doesn't relate to our everyday lives, but *Foundations* explodes that mold. This study makes it clear that the foundation of what we do and say in each day of our lives is what we believe. I am thrilled that this in-depth, life-changing curriculum is now being made available for everyone to use.

— Rick Warren, author of *The Purpose Driven® Life*

PREFACE

Get ready for a radical statement, a pronouncement sure to make you wonder if we've lost our grip on reality: *There is nothing more exciting than doctrine!*

Track with us for a second on this. Doctrine is the study of what God has to say. What God has to say is always the truth. The truth gives me the right perspective on myself and on the world around me. The right perspective results in decisions of faith and experiences of joy. *That* is exciting!

The objective of *Foundations* is to present the basic truths of the Christian faith in a simple, systematic, and life-changing way—in other words, to teach doctrine. The question is, why? In a world in which people's lives are filled with crying needs, why teach doctrine? Because biblical doctrine has the answer to many of those crying needs! Please don't see this as a clash between needs-oriented and doctrine-oriented teaching. The truth is we need both. We all need to learn how to deal with worry in our lives. One of the keys to dealing with worry is an understanding of the biblical doctrine of the hope of heaven. Couples need to know what the Bible says about how to have a better marriage. They also need a deeper understanding of the doctrine of the Fatherhood of God, giving the assurance of God's love upon which all healthy relationships are built. Parents need to understand the Bible's practical insights for raising kids. They also need an understanding of the sovereignty of God, a certainty of the fact that God is in control, that will carry them through the inevitable ups and downs of being a parent. Doctrinal truth meets our deepest needs.

Welcome to a study that will have a lifelong impact on the way you look at everything around you and above you and within you. Helping you develop a "Christian worldview" is our goal as the writers of this study. A Christian worldview is the ability to see everything through the filter of God's truth. The time you dedicate to this study will lay a foundation for new perspectives that will have tremendous benefits for the rest of your life. This study will help you:

- Lessen the stress in everyday life
- See the real potential for growth the Lord has given you
- Increase your sense of security in an often troubling world
- Find new tools for helping others (your friends, your family, your children) find the right perspective on life
- Fall more deeply in love with the Lord

Throughout this study you'll see three types of sidebar sections designed to help you connect with the truths God tells us about himself, ourselves, and this world.

- *A Closer Look:* We'll take time to expand on a truth or look at it from a different perspective.

- *A Fresh Word:* One aspect of doctrine that makes people nervous is the "big words." Throughout this study we'll take a fresh look at these words, words like *omnipotent* and *sovereign.*

- *Living on Purpose:* James 1:22 (NCV) says, *"Do what God's teaching says; when you only listen and do nothing, you are fooling yourselves."* In his book, *The Purpose Driven Life*, Rick Warren identifies God's five purposes for our lives. They are worship, fellowship, discipleship, ministry, and evangelism. We will focus on one of these five purposes in each lesson, and discuss how it relates to the subject of the study. This section is very important, so please be sure to leave time for it.

Here is a brief explanation of the other features of this study guide.

Looking Ahead/Catching Up: You will open each meeting with an opportunity for everyone to check in with each other about how you are doing with the weekly assignments. Accountability is a key to success in this study!

Key Verse: Each week you will find a key verse or Scripture passage for your group to read together. If someone in the group has a different translation, ask them to read it aloud so the group can get a bigger picture of the meaning of the passage.

Video Lesson: There is a video lesson segment for the group to watch together each week. Take notes in the lesson outlines as you watch the video, and be sure to refer back to these notes during your discussion time.

Discovery Questions: Each video segment is complemented by questions for group discussion. Please don't feel pressured to discuss every single question. The material in this study is meant to be your servant, not your master, so there is no reason to rush through the answers. Give everyone ample opportunity to share their thoughts. If you don't get through all of the discovery questions, that's okay.

Prayer Direction: At the end of each session you will find suggestions for your group prayer time. Praying together is one of the greatest privileges of small group life. Please don't take it for granted.

Get ready for God to do incredible things in your life as you begin the adventure of learning more deeply about the most exciting message in the world: the truth about God!

— Tom Holladay and Kay Warren

How to Use This Video Curriculum

Here is a brief explanation of the features on your small group DVD. These features include a *Group Lifter*, four *Video Teaching Sessions* by Tom Holladay and Kay Warren and a short video, *How to Become a Follower of Jesus Christ*, by Rick Warren. Here's how they work:

The *Group Lifter* is a brief video introduction by Tom Holladay giving you a sense of the objectives and purpose of this *Foundations* study on Creation. Watch it together as a group at the beginning of your first session.

The *Video Teaching Sessions* provide you with the teaching for each week of the study. Watch these features with your group. After watching the video teaching session, continue in your study by working through the discussion questions and activities in the study guide.

Nothing is more important than the decision you make to accept Jesus Christ as your Lord and Savior. You will have the option to watch a short video presentation, *How to Become a Follower of Jesus Christ*, at the end of Session Two. In this brief video segment, Rick Warren explains the importance of having Christ as the Savior of your life and how you can become part of the family of God. If everyone in your group is already a follower of Christ, or if you feel there is a better time to play this segment, continue your session by turning to the Discovery Questions in your DVD study guide. You can also select this video presentation separately on the Main Menu of the DVD for viewing at any time.

Follow these simple steps for a successful small group session:

1. Hosts: Watch the video session and write down your answers to the discussion questions before your group arrives.

2. Group: Open your group meeting by using the "Looking Ahead" or "Catching Up" section of your lesson.

3. Group: Watch the video teaching lesson and follow along in the outlines in the study guide.

4. Group: Complete the rest of the discussion materials for each session in the study guide.

It's just that simple. Have a great study together!

1

Session One

HOW DID GOD CREATE?

LOOKING AHEAD

1. What do you hope to get out of this small group study?

2. What is it that amazes you—simply amazes you—about God's creation?

Key Verse

You alone are the LORD. You made the heavens, even the highest heavens, and all their starry host, the earth and all that is on it, the seas and all that is in them. You give life to everything, and the multitudes of heaven worship you.

Nehemiah 9:6 (NIV)

BIBLE TEACHING
Watch the video lesson now and take notes in your outline on pages 3–6.

What You Believe about Your Origin Affects:

Your _____

Your _____

How you _____ God

Why Did God Create?

1. God created for his _____ .

   > *All things were created by him and for him.* (Colossians 1:16b NIV)

2. God created to express his _____ .

   > *The earth is the Lord's and everything in it, the world, and all who live in it.* (Psalm 24:1 NIV)

3. God created to reflect his _____ .

   > *From the time the world was created, people have seen the earth and sky and all that God made. They can clearly see his invisible qualities—his eternal power and divine nature. So they have no excuse whatsoever for not knowing God.* (Romans 1:20 NLT)

   You will find the verses Kay refers to on page 53 of this DVD study guide.

4. God created to show his _____ .

> *By wisdom the Lord laid the earth's foundations, by understanding he set the heavens in place.* (Proverbs 3:19 NIV)

> *Then he opened their minds so they could understand the Scriptures.* (Luke 24:45 NIV)

How Did God Create?

Evolution

This is not a view of "creation" because evolution does not involve a creator. In simplest terms, the view of evolution is that life originated from natural processes, beginning with the first living substance (a single cell) and continuing with the evolving of species.

It is impossible to prove _____ any theory of origins. This is because the scientific method is based on _____ and _____ .

Evolution and creation are not just a matter of _____ and _____ .

The problems with the theory of evolution:

1. God is _____ of creation.

Darwin himself rejected the idea of adding intervention by God into the concept of evolution:

> I will give absolutely nothing for the theory of natural selection if it requires miraculous additions at any one stage of descent.[1]

---

[1] R.E.D. Clark, *Darwin: Before and After* (London: Paternoster, 1948), 86.

2. The probability of evolution by _____ .

> It requires an incredible amount of faith to believe that evolution could have caused by chance all life that ever did or does now exist.[2]
>
> — Charles C. Ryrie

> The current scenario of the origin of life is about as likely as the assemblage of a 747 by a tornado whirling through a junkyard.[3]
>
> — Fred Hoyle

3. The lack of evidence for _____ evolution.

Charles Darwin concedes this lack of evidence in his writings:

> Not one change of species into another is on record . . . we cannot prove that a single species has been changed.[4]

The Bible tells us that God made each animal "after its kind." This is easily verified not only by the fossil record by also by modern scientific observation and experimentation. Animal breeders have successfully created new breeds of animals but have never changed one species into another.

> We are now about 120 years after Darwin, and knowledge of the fossil record has been greatly expanded. Ironically, we have even fewer examples of evolutionary transition than we had in Darwin's time. By this I mean that some of the classic cases of Darwinian change in the fossil record, such as the evolution of the horse in North America, have had to be discarded or modified as a result of more detailed information.[5]
>
> — David Raup

[2]Charles C. Ryrie, *Basic Theology* (Wheaton, Ill.: SP Publications, 1986), 177.

[3]Fred Hoyle, *The Intelligent Universe* (New York: Holt, Rinehart and Winston, 1983), 19.

[4]Francis Darwin, *Life and Letters of Charles Darwin* (New York: Basic Books, 1959), 1:210.

[5]David Raup, "Conflicts Between Darwin and Paleontology," *Field Museum of Natural History Bulletin* 30, no. 1 (1979): 25.

4. The irreducible _____ of living things.

> By irreducibly complex I mean a single system composed
> of several well-matched, interacting parts that contribute to
> the basic function, wherein the removal of any one of the
> parts causes the system to effectively cease functioning . . . .
> An irreducibly complex biological system, if there is such a
> thing, would be a powerful challenge to Darwinian evolution.[6]
>
> — Michael J. Behe

DISCOVERY QUESTIONS

1. One of the statements at the beginning of this study was, "What you
   believe about your origin affects your self-worth, your relationships,
   and how you view God." In what ways do you feel that your view of
   God as our Creator impacts your daily thoughts about yourself and
   this world?

2. How do you feel about the statement, "God created for his own
   sake?" How would you answer someone who says it would have
   been selfish of God to create for his own sake?

---

[6]Michael J. Behe, *Darwin's Black Box: The Biochemical Challenge to Evolution* (New York: Free Press,
1995), 39.

3. Where do you see God's wisdom? With your group, make a list of ways creation shows the wisdom of God.

Did You Get It? How has this week's study helped you see the significance of God's choice to create?

Share with Someone: Think of a person you can encourage with the truth you learned in this session. Write their name in the space below and pray for God to provide that opportunity this week.

LIVING ON PURPOSE

Worship

The Bible is filled with verses that tell us creation is an expression of God's character. To look more deeply into this, take some time before the next session to read the following verses and record your thoughts. Consider sharing one meaningful thought with the group at the next session.

- Nehemiah 9:5-6
- Psalm 8:1, 3
- Psalm 19:1-4
- Psalm 104:24
- Psalm 104:30-32
- Isaiah 43:7
- Isaiah 51:12-13, 16
- Amos 4:13
- Romans 1:20
- 2 Corinthians 4:6

PRAYER DIRECTION

Take some time as a group to talk about your specific prayer requests and to pray for one another.

Session two

2

SUPERNATURAL CREATION

CATCHING UP

1. Who did you share last week's truth with?

2. Last week's purpose activity gave you the opportunity to look up some verses regarding how God's character is revealed through creation. Take a couple minutes for those who did the exercise to share one meaningful thought they gained from this time in God's Word.

Key Verse

The heavens tell the glory of God, and the skies
announce what his hands have made.

Psalm 19:1 (NCV)

BIBLE TEACHING
Watch the video lesson now and take notes in your outline on pages 11–16.

How Did God Create? (Continued)

Theistic Evolution

Theistic evolution is the idea that God somehow used the process of evolution as the means by which he created everything.

Although this view is attractive to all who want to integrate the discoveries of science with the Bible, there are some significant problems with the idea of theistic evolution.

1. The Bible pictures God as being intimately and actively _____ in each aspect and moment of creation.

> *The heavens tell the glory of God, and the skies announce what his hands have made.* (Psalm 19:1 NCV)

> *You alone are the LORD. You made the heavens, even the highest heavens, and all their starry host, the earth and all that is on it, the seas and all that is in them. You give life to everything, and the multitudes of heaven worship you.* (Nehemiah 9:6 NIV)

> The problem with any form of theistic evolution . . . is that it means design by chance. That's like a square circle. There is no such thing. Blending evolution with creation is like putting a square peg in a round hole. It just doesn't fit.[1]
>
> — Gregory Koukl

---

[1] Gregory Koukl, *Michael Behe's Theistic Evolution*, transcript of Stand to Reason Radio, 24 December 1997, accessed 1 February 2003 at www.str.org.

2. A _____ rather than _____ view of Genesis 1–11.

> We must realize that the book of Genesis is the foundation of the entire Bible. The word Genesis means "beginnings." Genesis tells the story of the beginning of the universe, solar system, earth, life, man, sin, Israel, nations, and salvation. An understanding of Genesis is crucial to our understanding of the rest of Scripture.
>
> For example, Genesis chapters 1–11 are quoted or referred to more than 100 times in the New Testament alone. And it is over these chapters that the primary battle for the historicity of Genesis rages. All of the first eleven chapters are referred to in the New Testament. Every New Testament author refers somewhere to Genesis 1–11. . . .
>
> How can the first 11 chapters be separated from even the rest of Genesis? The time of Abraham has been verified by archeology. The places, customs, and religions spoken of in Genesis related to Abraham are accurate. The story of Abraham begins in Genesis 12. If Genesis 1 is mythology and Genesis 12 is history, where does the allegory stop and the history begin in the first 11 chapters? It is all written in the same historical narrative style.[2]
>
> — Dr. Ray Bohlin

3. Placing God's _____ and God's _____ on equal footing as revelations of God.

While the heavens do "tell the glory of God," they cannot do so as faithfully and clearly as the Bible.

> *The grass withers and the flowers fall, but the word of our God stands forever.* (Isaiah 40:8 NIV)

> *"Heaven and earth will pass away, but my words will never pass away."* (Matthew 24:35 NIV)

---

[2]Dr. Ray Bohlin, *Why We Believe in Creation*. Accessed 1 February 2003 at www.probe.org.

Supernatural Creation

God _____ and _____ created the heavens and the earth.

Science may provide reasonable evidence, but ultimately it is a matter of faith.

1. Science shows us the big bang, but it takes _____ to believe God said, *"Let there be light."* (Genesis 1:3 NIV)

   Science can point to a creator:

   On May 4, 1992, *Time* magazine reported that NASA's Cosmic Background Explorer satellite—COBE—had discovered landmark evidence that the universe did in fact begin with the primeval explosion that has become known as the Big Bang. "If you're religious, it's like looking at God," proclaimed the leader of the research team, George Smoot.[3]

   But only by faith can we believe in our Creator:

   In Genesis 1:3 the Bible says, *"And God said, 'Let there be light,' and there was light."* (NIV)

2. Science shows us the intelligent design of the universe, but it takes faith to believe God _____ that universe.

   Science can point to a creator:

   A July 20, 1998, *Newsweek* article entitled "Science Finds God" reported:

   > Physicists have stumbled on signs that the cosmos is custom-made for life and consciousness. It turns out that if the constants of nature—unchanging numbers like the

---

[3]Michael D. Lemonick, "Echoes of the Big Bang," *Time* (4 May 1992): 62.

strength of gravity, the charge of an electron and the mass of a proton—were the tiniest bit different, then atoms would not hold together, stars would not burn and life would never have made an appearance. "When you realize that the laws of nature must be incredibly finely tuned to produce the universe we see," says John Polkinghorne, who had a distinguished career as a physicist at Cambridge University before becoming an Anglican priest in 1982, "that conspires to plant the idea that the universe did not just happen, but that there must be a purpose behind it." Charles Townes, who shared the 1965 Nobel Prize in Physics for discovering the principles of the laser, goes further: "Many have a feeling that somehow intelligence must have been involved in the laws of the universe."[4]

But only by faith can we believe in our Creator:

In Genesis 1:1 the Bible says, *"In the beginning God created the heavens and the earth."* (NIV)

A sound explanation may exist for the explosive birth of our Universe; but if it does, science cannot find out what the explanation is. The scientist's pursuit of the past ends in the moment of creation. This is an exceedingly strange development, unexpected by all but the theologians. They have always accepted the word of the Bible: In the beginning God created heaven and earth. . . . For the scientist who has lived by his faith in the power of reason, the story ends like a bad dream. He has scaled the mountains of ignorance; he is about to conquer the highest peak; as he pulls himself over the final rock, he is greeted by a band of theologians who have been sitting there for centuries.[5]

— Robert Jastrow, founder of NASA's
Goddard Institute for Space Studies

---

[4]Sharon Begley, "Science Finds God," *Newsweek* (20 July 1998): 46–51.

[5]Robert Jastrow, *God and the Astronomers*, 2d ed. (New York: W.W. Norton, 1992), 106–7.

When Did God Create?

1. All evolutionists believe that Earth is _____ of years old.

2. Creationists are divided; most believe in a _____ ,
   but there are some who believe in an _____ .

The debate between these views centers around the translation of the word *day* (*yom* in Hebrew) in the Genesis 1 text. *Yom* can mean any of the following:

- A 24-hour day, which is the most common usage in the Old Testament

- An unspecified period of time

- An era

A CLOSER LOOK

Two Questions

1. How could "old earth" creationists believe that the earth is billions of years old when the Bible says that God created it in just six days?

   They believe that the days detailed in Genesis 1 represent millions of years or that there was a significant gap between the days of creation.

2. How could "young earth" creationists believe that the earth is thousands of years old in light of the scientific evidence?

   They believe that God created the universe in full working order—with starlight already reaching the earth and the ecosystem fully mature. They believe that this fact (along with the cataclysm caused by a worldwide flood) calls into question the apparent time lines deduced from radioactive dating, the earth's magnetic field, petroleum gas deposits, planet rotations, etc.

When did sin and death enter the world?

The major theological question concerning when God created is, "When did sin and death enter the world?"

Since . . .

The Bible tells us that it was Adam's personal choice to sin that brought death and the fall of creation.

> *When Adam sinned, sin entered the entire human race. Adam's sin brought death, so death spread to everyone, for everyone sinned.* (Romans 5:12 NLT)

Romans 8:20 tells us that the whole creation suffers because of Adam's sin. One sin infected all of creation.

And since . . .

The salvation that Jesus brings to us is tied in the New Testament to the historical fact of Adam's sin.

> [21]*For since death came through a man, the resurrection of the dead comes also through a man.* [22]*For as in Adam all die, so in Christ all will be made alive.* (1 Corinthians 15:21–22 NIV)

Therefore . . .

Any idea of creation that theorizes the death of human beings and the fall of God's creation before the sin of Adam and Eve is contrary to the clear teaching of God's Word.

"HOW TO BECOME A FOLLOWER OF JESUS CHRIST"

Have you ever surrendered your life to Jesus Christ? Take a few minutes with your group to watch a brief video by Pastor Rick Warren on how to become part of the family of God. It is included on the Main Menu of this DVD.

Discovery Questions

1. What aspects of creation make God seem the most personal to you? How does observing his creation encourage you to love and trust him more?

2. What have you heard so far in our teaching on creation that has been the most helpful for you in your personal, everyday life? Has this study of creation changed the way you view something or someone? Share that new perspective with the group.

3. Does a discussion of topics such as irreducible complexity and fossil records excite you or bore you to tears? Why do you think people differ on this point: why do some love to study these details while others could happily do without them?

4. How can we discuss creation in such a way that we don't appear scientifically illiterate? What are some ways we can express to others that we are not ignoring the seeming evidence, we are simply seeing it differently?

Did You Get It? How has this week's study helped you see the importance to your life and your family of the creation/evolution debate?

Share with Someone: Think of a person you can encourage with the truth you learned in this session. Write their name in the space below and pray for God to provide that opportunity this week.

LIVING ON PURPOSE

Ministry

What one thing could you do to advance the idea of God as Creator and God's Word as vastly more reliable than the idea of evolution? In your community? With other believers? In your own family?

PRAYER DIRECTION

Take some time to praise God together in your group prayer time. Try praying "conversationally." When you pray conversationally, you talk to God together as you would talk in a normal conversation. Instead of taking "turns" and praying once about everything that's on your mind, talk to God about one subject with everyone adding a sentence or comment of prayer. When you've prayed about that subject for a while, someone will introduce a different subject as you pray, and you all chime in on that with a sentence or comment to the Lord. Talk to God as one who is right there in the room with you—a part of the conversation.

3

Session three

TRUTHS ABOUT CREATION

CATCHING UP

1. Who did you share last week's truth with?

2. What did you learn about creation during last week's purpose activity? Did anyone apply the ideas discussed in what one thing you could do to advance God as Creator over evolution?

3. God has given us so much to enjoy on earth. Share some things you simply enjoy in his creation.

Key Verse

By faith we understand that the universe was formed at God's command, so that what is seen was not made out of what was visible.

Hebrews 11:3 (NIV)

Seven Truths about Creation That Are Foundations for Our Lives, Part 1

One: God created everything out of _____.

By faith we understand that the universe was formed at God's command, so that what is seen was not made out of what was visible. (Hebrews 11:3 NIV)

And God said, "Let there be light," and there was light. (Genesis 1:3 NIV)

God simply spoke and creation happened.

Two: Creation was done in _____.

³And God said, "Let there be light. . . . ⁸God called the expanse "sky" . . . ⁹"Let the water under the sky be gathered to one place, and let dry ground appear. . . . ¹¹Let the land produce vegetation . . ." ¹²The land produced vegetation: plants bearing seed according to their kinds and trees bearing fruit with seed in it according to their kinds. . . . ¹⁴"Let there be lights in the expanse of the sky to separate the day from the night, and let them serve as signs to mark seasons and days and years. . . . ²⁰Let the water teem with living creatures, and let birds fly above the earth. . . . ²⁴Let the land produce living creatures according to their kinds. . . . ²⁶Let us make man in our image . . ." (Genesis 1:3–26 NIV)

Different Views

- Both evolutionists and creationists believe in a _____ creation.

- Evolution is the idea that order evolved out of _____ .

- The Bible teaches instead that order was created by _____ .

Three: God saw that it was _____ .

God saw all that he had made, and it was very good. And there was evening, and there was morning—the sixth day. (Genesis 1:31 NIV)

Creation: Good or Evil?

- God's creation is _____ . The world did not make people evil: people brought evil into the world.

- Don't make the mistake of thinking that because something is of the _____ it must therefore be evil.

. . . God richly gives us everything to enjoy. (1 Timothy 6:17 NCV)

Four: Man is the _____ .

How exactly did God create man?

Then the Lord God took dust from the ground and formed a man from it. He breathed the breath of life into the man's nose, and the man became a living person. (Genesis 2:7 NCV)

[21]So the Lord God caused the man to sleep very deeply, and while he was asleep, God removed one of the man's ribs. Then God closed up the man's skin at the place where he took the rib. [22]The Lord God used the rib from the man to make a woman, and then he brought the woman to the man. (Genesis 2:21–22 NCV)

DISCOVERY QUESTIONS

1. In what ways does God's creation speak to you specifically about the person and character of God? (Example: when I look at the stars . . . at the ocean . . . at the Grand Canyon, etc.)

2. Some people take extreme views when it comes to material things, seeing them as either "good" or "evil." How do you see material things? Discuss within your group the difference between recognizing that evil is present in this world and thinking that everything that is material must be evil.

3. Often the realities of our lives can easily overwhelm us and cause us to take our focus off of God. How can the truth about creation fill you with wonder again and be a constant reminder that God has a plan for you and this world?

Did You Get It? How has this week's study helped you see how the truth of creation impacts your everyday attitudes?

Share with Someone: Think of a person you can encourage with the truth you learned in this session. Write their name in the space below and pray for God to provide that opportunity this week.

LIVING ON PURPOSE
Worship

Some of the greatest songs of praise are written to God as our Creator. Before you leave, remind yourselves of some of those great songs and hymns by singing together, reading the words, or listening to such Christian songs as:

How Great Thou Art

O Lord my God, When I in awesome wonder
Consider all the worlds Thy hands have made
I see the stars, I hear the rolling thunder
Thy pow'r throughout the universe displayed

(Chorus)
Then sings my soul, my Savior God to Thee
How great Thou art, how great Thou art
Then sings my soul, my Savior God to Thee
How great Thou art, how great Thou art

When through the woods, and forest glades I wander
And hear the birds sing sweetly in the trees
When I look down, from lofty mountain grandeur
And hear the brook and feel the gentle breeze

Chorus

And when I think that God His Son not sparing
Sent Him to die, I scarce can take it in
That on the cross, my burden gladly bearing
He bled and died to take away my sin

Chorus

When Christ shall come with shout of acclamation
And take me home, what joy shall fill my heart
Then I shall bow in humble adoration
And there proclaim, "My God, how great Thou art"

Chorus

God of Wonders

Lord of all creation
Of water, earth and sky
The heavens are Your tabernacle
Glory to the Lord on high

(Chorus)
God of wonders beyond our galaxy
You are holy, holy
The universe declares your majesty
You are holy, holy
Lord of heaven and earth
Lord of heaven and earth

Early in the morning
I will celebrate the light
And when I stumble into darkness
I will call your name by night

Chorus

Hallelujah to the Lord of heaven and earth
Hallelujah to the Lord of heaven and earth
Hallelujah to the Lord of heaven and earth

(Chorus 2)
God of wonders beyond our galaxy
You are holy, holy
Precious Lord, reveal your heart to me
Father hold me, hold me
The universe declares your majesty
You are holy, holy

Indescribable

From the highest of heights to the depths of the sea
Creation's revealing Your majesty
From the colors of fall to the fragrance of spring
Every creature unique in the song that it sings
All exclaiming

(Chorus)
Indescribable, uncontainable
You placed the stars in the sky
And You know them by name
You are amazing God
All powerful, untamable
Awestruck we fall to our knees
As we humbly proclaim
You are amazing God

Who has told ev'ry lightning bolt where it should go
Or seen heavenly storehouses laden with snow
Who imagined the sun and gives source to its light
Yet conceals it to bring us the coolness of night
None can fathom

Chorus (3x)

PRAYER DIRECTION

Take some time as a group to talk about your specific prayer requests and to pray for one another.

Session four

4

MORE TRUTHS ABOUT CREATION

CATCHING UP

1. Who did you share last week's truth with?

2. What did you learn about creation during last week's purpose activity, as you worshiped the God of creation?

Key Verse

He existed before everything else began, and he holds all creation together.
Colossians 1:17 (NLT)

BIBLE TEACHING
Watch the video lesson now and take notes in your outline on pages 29–31.

Seven Truths about Creation
That Are Foundations for Our Lives, Part 2

Man is the Crown of Creation *(Continued)*

How are we created in God's image?

- Our _____ : mind, will, emotions

- Our _____ : created as male and female

> *So God created man in his own image, in the image*
> *of God he created him; male and female he created them.*
> (Genesis 1:27 NIV)

A CLOSER LOOK
Made in the Image of God

Because all mankind was made in the image of God:

Both _____ and _____ have equal value and worth.

Each _____ has equal value and worth.

> [26]*From one man he made every nation of men, that they should inhabit the whole earth; and he determined the times set for them and the exact places where they should live.* [27]*God did this so that men would seek him and perhaps reach out for him and find him, though he is not far from each one of us.* [28]*"For in him we live and move and have our being."*
> (Acts 17:26–28 NIV)

- Our _____ : created as moral beings, with a moral consciousness

  Then the eyes of both of them were opened, and they realized they were naked; so they sewed fig leaves together and made coverings for themselves. (Genesis 3:7 NIV)

  So I strive always to keep my conscience clear before God and man. (Acts 24:16 NIV)

Our moral nature includes both freedom of choice and responsibility for our choices.

- Our _____ : created with the ability to relate to God

  Now we rejoice in our wonderful new relationship with God— all because of what our Lord Jesus Christ has done in dying for our sins—making us friends of God. (Romans 5:11 LB)

Five: God _____ the job.

Thus the heavens and earth were completed in all their vast array. (Genesis 2:1 NIV)

. . . God's work was finished from the time he made the world. (Hebrews 4:3 NCV)

- The universe is not some vast unfinished symphony.

- This world and universe are not works in progress.

- The universe is a finished work of creation that has been marred by the presence of sin.

Six: God _____ on the seventh day.

[2]By the seventh day God had finished the work he had been doing; so on the seventh day he rested from all his work. [3]And God blessed the seventh day and made it holy, because on it he rested from all the work of creating that he had done. (Genesis 2:2–3 NIV)

Why did God rest?

- To give us an _____ to follow

  ⁹Work and get everything done during six days each week, ¹⁰but the seventh day is a day of rest to honor the Lord your God. . . . ¹¹The reason is that in six days the Lord made everything—the sky, the earth, the sea, and everything in them. On the seventh day he rested . . . (Exodus 20:9–11 NCV)

- To teach us his _____ for the ages

  ⁹There remains, then, a Sabbath-rest for the people of God; ¹⁰for anyone who enters God's rest also rests from his own work, just as God did from his. ¹¹Let us, therefore, make every effort to enter that rest . . . (Hebrews 4:9–11 NIV)

Seven: God now _____ all that he made.

  He existed before everything else began, and he holds all creation together. (Colossians 1:17 NLT)

A FRESH WORD
Providence

Providence is the word used to describe God's continuing and active work in holding creation together. Never make the mistake of thinking that God made it all and then somehow left it to run on its own. There are literally hundreds of verses throughout the Bible concerning God's intimate and intricate sustaining of his creation. From the smallest dewdrop to the greatest nations, God sustains it all!

Who fathers the drops of dew? (Job 38:28b NIV)

God reigns over the nations; God is seated on his holy throne. (Psalm 47:8 NIV)

DISCOVERY QUESTIONS

1. Which of the four aspects of our being created in God's image (personality, sexuality, morality, and spirituality) seems most significant to you at this point in your life?

2. How does the fact that we are created in God's image inspire you to "raise the bar" on the goals you have for your life?

3. How well are you doing at following God's example to rest? Discuss one or two practical things you could do to better follow his example.

Did You Get It? How has this week's study helped you to see how the truth of creation makes a difference every day of our lives? How can you take this truth and bring it into your life this week?

Share with Someone: Think of a person you can encourage with the truth you learned in this session. Write their name in the space below and pray for God to provide that opportunity this week.

LIVING ON PURPOSE
Discipleship

Three or four times during your quiet time this week, end by praying this simple prayer. With each phrase, read these accompanying verses.

"Seeing creation as an expression of your love . . . "

⁷He made the sun and the moon. His love continues forever. ⁸He made the sun to rule the day. His love continues forever. ⁹He made the moon and stars to rule the night. His love continues forever . . . ²⁵He gives food to every living creature. His love continues forever. (Psalm 136:7-9, 25 NCV)

"I kneel before you in humility . . . "

⁶Come, kneel before the Lord our Maker, ⁷for he is our God. We are his sheep, and he is our Shepherd. Oh, that you would hear him calling you today and come to him! (Psalm 95:6-7 LB)

"praising you for this day . . . "

This is the day the Lord has made; let us rejoice and be glad in it. (Psalm 118:24 NIV)

"and thanking you for creating me."

I praise you because you made me in an amazing and wonderful way. What you have done is wonderful. I know this very well. (Psalm 139:14 NCV)

PRAYER DIRECTION

Pray a prayer of praise together tonight based on the truths God tells us in Genesis 1. Do this by having someone read a day of creation, and then have the group pray and praise God for the truths in those verses. After a few moments, have the next person around the circle read the next day of creation, and spend a few moments talking to God about your gratefulness for the truths in those verses.

(You will find the days of creation listed below in *The Message* paraphrase. Read these verses in its contemporary language to give you a fresh perspective on this familiar Bible passage.)

Day 1

> *First this: God created the Heavens and Earth—all you see, all you don't see. ²Earth was a soup of nothingness, a bottomless emptiness, an inky blackness. God's Spirit brooded like a bird above the watery abyss. ³God spoke: "Light!" And light appeared. ⁴God saw that light was good and separated light from dark. ⁵God named the light Day, he named the dark Night. It was evening, it was morning—Day One.* (Genesis 1:1–5 MSG)

Day 2

> *⁶God spoke: "Sky! In the middle of the waters; separate water from water!" ⁷God made sky. He separated the water under sky from the water above sky. And there it was: ⁸he named sky the Heavens; It was evening, it was morning—Day Two.* (Genesis 1:6–8 MSG)

Day 3

> *⁹God spoke: "Separate! Water-beneath-Heaven, gather into one place; Land, appear!" And there it was. ¹⁰God named the land Earth. He named the pooled water Ocean. God saw that it was good. ¹¹God spoke: "Earth, green up! Grow all varieties of seed-bearing plants, every sort of fruit-bearing tree." And there it was. ¹²Earth produced green seed-bearing plants, all varieties, and fruit-bearing trees of all sorts. God saw that it was good. ¹³It was evening, it was morning—Day Three.* (Genesis 1:9–13 MSG)

Day 4

¹⁴God spoke: "Lights! Come out! Shine in Heaven's sky! Separate Day from Night. Mark seasons and days and years, ¹⁵lights in Heaven's sky to give light to Earth." And there it was. ¹⁶God made two big lights, the larger to take charge of Day, the smaller to be in charge of Night; and he made the stars. ¹⁷God placed them in the heavenly sky to light up Earth ¹⁸and oversee Day and Night, to separate light and dark. God saw that it was good. ¹⁹It was evening, it was morning—Day Four. (Genesis 1:14–19 MSG)

Day 5

²⁰God spoke: "Swarm, Ocean, with fish and all sea life! Birds, fly through the sky over Earth!" ²¹God created the huge whales, all the swarm of life in the waters, and every kind and species of flying birds. God saw that it was good. ²²God blessed them: "Prosper! Reproduce! Fill Ocean! Birds, reproduce on Earth!" ²³It was evening, it was morning—Day Five. (Genesis 1:20–23 MSG)

Day 6

²⁴God spoke: "Earth, generate life! Every sort and kind: cattle and reptiles and wild animals—all kinds." And there it was: ²⁵wild animals of every kind, cattle of all kinds, every sort of reptile and bug. God saw that it was good. ²⁶God spoke: "Let us make human beings in our image, make them reflecting our nature so they can be responsible for the fish in the sea, the birds in the air, the cattle, and, yes, Earth itself, and every animal that moves on the face of Earth." ²⁷God created human beings; he created them godlike, reflecting God's nature. He created them male and female. ²⁸God blessed them: "Prosper! Reproduce! Fill Earth! Take charge! Be responsible for fish in the sea and birds in the air, for every living thing that moves on the face of Earth."

²⁹Then God said, "I've given you every sort of seed-bearing plant on Earth and every kind of fruit-bearing tree, given them to you for food. ³⁰To all animals and all birds, everything that moves and breathes, I give whatever grows out of the ground for food." And there it was. [31]*God looked over everything he had made; it was so good, so very good! It was evening, it was morning—Day Six.* (Genesis 1:24–31 MSG)

Day 7

[1]*Heaven and Earth were finished, down to the last detail.* [2]*By the seventh day God had finished his work. On the seventh day he rested from all his work.* [3]*God blessed the seventh day. He made it a Holy Day because on that day he rested from his work, all the creating God had done.* (Genesis 2:1–3 MSG)

Small Group Resources

HELPS FOR HOSTS

Top Ten Ideas for New Hosts

Congratulations! As the host of your small group, you have responded to the call to help shepherd Jesus' flock. Few other tasks in the family of God surpass the contribution you will be making.

As you prepare to facilitate your group, whether it is one session or the entire series, here are a few thoughts to keep in mind. We encourage you to read and review these tips with each new discussion host before he or she leads.

Remember you are not alone. God knows everything about you, and he knew you would be asked to facilitate your group. Even though you may not feel ready, this is common for all good hosts. God promises, *"I will never leave you; I will never abandon you"* (Hebrews 13:5 TEV). Whether you are facilitating for one evening, several weeks, or a lifetime, you will be blessed as you serve.

1. **Don't try to do it alone.** Pray right now for God to help you build a healthy team. If you can enlist a cohost to help you shepherd the group, you will find your experience much richer. This is your chance to involve as many people as you can in building a healthy group. All you have to do is ask people to help. You'll be surprised at the response.

2. **Be friendly and be yourself.** God wants to use your unique gifts and temperament. Be sure to greet people at the door with a big smile . . . this can set the mood for the whole gathering. Remember, they are taking as big a step to show up at your house as you are to lead this group! Don't try to do things exactly like another host; do them in a way that fits you. Admit when you don't have an answer and apologize when you make a mistake. Your group will love you for it and you'll sleep better at night.

3. **Prepare for your meeting ahead of time.** Review the session and write down your responses to each question. Pay special attention to exercises that ask group members to do something other than engage in discussion. These exercises will help your group live what the Bible teaches, not just talk about it. Be sure you understand how an exercise works. If the exercise employs one of the items in the Small Group Resources section (such as the Group Guidelines), be sure to look over that item so you'll know how it works.

4. **Pray for your group members by name.** Before you begin your session, take a few moments and pray for each member by name. You may want to review the prayer list at least once a week. Ask God to use your time together to touch the heart of every person in your group. Expect God to lead you to whomever he wants you to encourage or challenge in a special way. If you listen, God will surely lead.

5. **When you ask a question, be patient.** Someone will eventually respond. Sometimes people need a moment or two of silence to think about the question. If silence doesn't bother you, it won't bother anyone else. After someone responds, affirm the response with a simple "thanks" or "great answer." Then ask, "How about somebody else?" or "Would someone who hasn't shared like to add anything?" Be sensitive to new people or reluctant members who aren't ready to say, pray, or do anything. If you give them a safe setting, they will blossom over time. If someone in your group is a "wallflower" who sits silently through every session, consider talking to them privately and encouraging them to participate. Let them know how important they are to you—that they are loved and appreciated—and that the group would value their input. Remember, still water often runs deep.

6. **Provide transitions between questions.** Ask if anyone would like to read the paragraph or Bible passage. Don't call on anyone, but ask for a volunteer, and then be patient until someone begins. Be sure to thank the person who reads aloud.

7. **Break into smaller groups occasionally.** With a greater opportunity to talk in a small circle, people will connect more with the study, apply more quickly what they're learning, and ultimately get more out of their small group experience. A small circle also encourages a quiet person to participate and tends to minimize the effects of a more vocal or dominant member.

8. **Small circles are also helpful during prayer time.** People who are unaccustomed to praying aloud will feel more comfortable trying it with just two or three others. Also, prayer requests won't take as much time, so circles will have more time to actually pray. When you gather back with the whole group, you can have one person from each circle briefly update everyone on the prayer requests from their subgroups. The other great aspect of subgrouping is that it fosters leadership development. As you ask people in the group to facilitate discussion or to lead a prayer circle, it gives them a small leadership step that can build their confidence.

9. **Rotate facilitators occasionally.** You may be perfectly capable of hosting each time, but you will help others grow in their faith and gifts if you give them opportunities to host the group.

10. **One final challenge (for new or first-time hosts).** Before your first opportunity to lead, look up each of the six passages that follow. Read each one as a devotional exercise to help prepare you with a shepherd's heart. Trust us on this one. If you do this, you will be more than ready for your first meeting.

Matthew 9:36–38 (NIV)
36When Jesus saw the crowds, he had compassion on them, because they were harassed and helpless, like sheep without a shepherd. 37Then he said to his disciples, "The harvest is plentiful but the workers are few. 38Ask the Lord of the harvest, therefore, to send out workers into his harvest field."

John 10:14–15 (NIV)
14I am the good shepherd; I know my sheep and my sheep know me—15just as the Father knows me and I know the Father—and I lay down my life for the sheep.

1 Peter 5:2–4 (NIV)

²Be shepherds of God's flock that is under your care, serving as overseers—not because you must, but because you are willing, as God wants you to be; ³not greedy for money, but eager to serve; not lording it over those entrusted to you, but being examples to the flock. ⁴And when the Chief Shepherd appears, you will receive the crown of glory that will never fade away.

Philippians 2:1–5 (NIV)

¹If you have any encouragement from being united with Christ, if any comfort from his love, if any fellowship with the Spirit, if any tenderness and compassion, ²then make my joy complete by being like-minded, having the same love, being one in spirit and purpose. ³Do nothing out of selfish ambition or vain conceit, but in humility consider others better than yourselves. ⁴Each of you should look not only to your own interests, but also to the interests of others. ⁵Your attitude should be the same as that of Jesus Christ.

Hebrews 10:23–25 (NIV)

²³Let us hold unswervingly to the hope we profess, for he who promised is faithful. ²⁴And let us consider how we may spur one another on toward love and good deeds. ²⁵Let us not give up meeting together, as some are in the habit of doing, but let us encourage one another—and all the more as you see the Day approaching.

1 Thessalonians 2:7–8, 11–12 (NIV)

⁷. . . but we were gentle among you, like a mother caring for her little children. ⁸We loved you so much that we were delighted to share with you not only the gospel of God but our lives as well, because you had become so dear to us. . . . ¹¹For you know that we dealt with each of you as a father deals with his own children, ¹²encouraging, comforting and urging you to live lives worthy of God, who calls you into his kingdom and glory.

FREQUENTLY ASKED QUESTIONS

How long will this group meet?

This volume of *Foundations: Creation* is four sessions long. We encourage your group to add a fifth session for a celebration. In your final session, each group member may decide if he or she desires to continue on for another study. At that time you may also want to do some informal evaluation, discuss your Group Guidelines, and decide which study you want to do next. We recommend you visit our website at **www.saddlebackresources.com** for more video-based small group studies.

Who is the host?

The host is the person who coordinates and facilitates your group meetings. In addition to a host, we encourage you to select one or more group members to lead your group discussions. Several other responsibilities can be rotated, including refreshments, prayer requests, worship, or keeping up with those who miss a meeting. Shared ownership in the group helps everybody grow.

Where do we find new group members?

Recruiting new members can be a challenge for groups, especially new groups with just a few people, or existing groups that lose a few people along the way. We encourage you to use the *Circles of Life* diagram on page 46 of this DVD study guide to brainstorm a list of people from your workplace, church, school, neighborhood, family, and so on. Then pray for the people on each member's list. Allow each member to invite several people from their list. Some groups fear that newcomers will interrupt the intimacy that members have built over time. However, groups that welcome newcomers generally gain strength with the infusion of new blood. Remember, the next person you add just might become a friend for eternity. Logistically, groups find different ways to add members. Some groups remain permanently open, while others choose to open periodically, such as at the beginning or end of a study. If your group becomes too large for easy, face-to-face conversations, you can subgroup, forming a second discussion group in another room.

How do we handle the child care needs in our group?

Child care needs must be handled very carefully. This is a sensitive issue. We suggest you seek creative solutions as a group. One common solution is to have the adults meet in the living room and share the cost of a babysitter (or two) who can be with the kids in another part of the house. Another popular option is to have one home for the kids and a second home (close by) for the adults. If desired, the adults could rotate the responsibility of providing a lesson for the kids. This last option is great with school-age kids and can be a huge blessing to families.

GROUP GUIDELINES

It's a good idea for every group to put words to their shared values, expectations, and commitments. Such guidelines will help you avoid unspoken agendas and unmet expectations. We recommend you discuss your guidelines during Session One in order to lay the foundation for a healthy group experience. Feel free to modify anything that does not work for your group.

We agree to the following values:

Clear Purpose	To grow healthy spiritual lives by building a healthy small group community
Group Attendance	To give priority to the group meeting (call if I am absent or late)
Safe Environment	To create a safe place where people can be heard and feel loved (no quick answers, snap judgments, or simple fixes)
Be Confidential	To keep anything that is shared strictly confidential and within the group
Conflict Resolution	To avoid gossip and to immediately resolve any concerns by following the principles of Matthew 18:15–17
Spiritual Health	To give group members permission to speak into my life and help me live a healthy, balanced spiritual life that is pleasing to God
Limit Our Freedom	To limit our freedom by not serving or consuming alcohol during small group meetings or events so as to avoid causing a weaker brother or sister to stumble (1 Corinthians 8:1–13; Romans 14:19–21)

GROUP GUIDELINES

Welcome Newcomers   To invite friends who might benefit from this study and warmly welcome newcomers

Building Relationships   To get to know the other members of the group and pray for them regularly

Other   _____

We have also discussed and agreed on the following items:

Child Care

_____

_____

Starting Time

_____

Ending Time

_____

If you haven't already done so, take a few minutes to fill out the *Small Group Calendar* on page 50.

CIRCLES OF LIFE—SMALL GROUP CONNECTIONS

Discover who you can connect in community

Use this chart to help carry out one of the values in the Group Guidelines to "Welcome Newcomers."

"Follow me, and I will make you fishers of men." (Matthew 4:19 KJV)

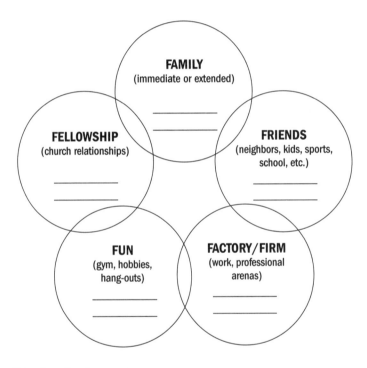

Follow this simple three-step process:

1. List 1–2 people in each circle.

2. Prayerfully select one person or couple from your list and tell your group about them.

3. Give them a call and invite them to your next meeting. Over 50 percent of those invited to a small group say, "Yes!"

SMALL GROUP PRAYER AND PRAISE REPORT

This is a place where you can write each other's requests for prayer. You can also make a note when God answers a prayer. Pray for each other's requests. If you're new to group prayer, it's okay to pray silently or to pray by using just one sentence: "God, please help

_____ to _____ ."

DATE	PERSON	PRAYER REQUEST	PRAISE REPORT

SMALL GROUP PRAYER AND PRAISE REPORT

DATE	PERSON	PRAYER REQUEST	PRAISE REPORT

SMALL GROUP PRAYER AND PRAISE REPORT

DATE	PERSON	PRAYER REQUEST	PRAISE REPORT

SMALL GROUP CALENDAR

Healthy groups share responsibilities and group ownership. It might take some time for this to develop. Shared ownership ensures that responsibility for the group doesn't fall to one person. Use the calendar to keep track of social events, mission projects, birthdays, or days off. Complete this calendar at your first or second meeting. Planning ahead will increase attendance and shared ownership.

DATE	LESSON	LOCATION	FACILITATOR	SNACK OR MEAL
5/4	Session 2	Chris and Andrea	Jim Brown	Phil and Karen

ANSWER KEY

Session One:
How Did God Create?

- Your <u>self-worth</u>
- Your <u>relationships</u>
- How you <u>view</u> God

1. God created for his <u>own sake</u>.
2. God created to express his <u>sovereignty</u>.
3. God created to reflect his <u>character</u>.
4. God created to show his <u>wisdom</u>.

It is impossible to prove <u>scientifically</u> any theory of origins. This is because the scientific method is based on <u>observation</u> and <u>experimentation</u>.

Evolution and creation are not just a matter of <u>science</u> and <u>religion</u>.

1. God is <u>left out</u> of creation.
2. The probability of evolution by <u>chance</u>.
3. The lack of evidence for <u>species-to-species</u>. evolution
4. The irreducible <u>complexity</u> of living things.

Session Two:
Supernatural Creation

1. The Bible pictures God as being intimately and actively <u>involved</u> in each aspect and moment of creation.
2. A <u>poetic</u> rather than <u>historical</u> view of Genesis 1–11.
3. Placing God's <u>creation</u> and God's <u>Word</u> on equal footing as revelations of God.

God <u>personally</u> and <u>supernaturally</u> created the heavens and the earth.

1. Science shows us the big bang, but it takes <u>faith</u> to believe God said, *"Let there be light."* (Genesis 1:3 NIV)
2. Science shows us the intelligent design of the universe, but it takes faith to believe God <u>personally created</u> that universe.

1. All evolutionists believe that Earth is <u>billions</u> of years old.
2. Creationists are divided; most believe in a <u>young earth</u>, but there are some who believe in an <u>old planet</u>.

Session Three:
Truths about Creation

One: God created everything out of <u>nothing</u>.

Two: Creation was done in <u>proper order</u>.

- Both evolutionists and creationists believe in a <u>well-ordered</u> creation.
- Evolution is the idea that order evolved out of <u>chaos</u>.
- The Bible teaches instead that order was created by <u>design</u>.

Three: God saw that it was <u>good</u>.

- God's creation is <u>not evil</u>.
- Don't make the mistake of thinking that because something is of the <u>physical world</u> it must therefore be evil.

Four: Man is the <u>Crown of Creation</u>.

Session Four:
More Truths about Creation

- Our <u>personality</u>: mind, will, emotions
- Our <u>sexuality</u>: created as male and female

Both <u>male</u> and <u>female</u> have equal value and worth.

Each <u>race</u> has equal value and worth.

- Our <u>morality</u>: created as moral beings, with a moral consciousness
- Our <u>spirituality</u>: created with the ability to relate to God

Five: God <u>finished</u> the job.

Six: God <u>rested</u> on the seventh day.

- To give us an <u>example</u> to follow
- To teach us his <u>plan</u> for the ages

Seven: God now <u>sustains</u> all that he made.

NOTES

KEY VERSES

One of the most effective ways to drive deeply into our lives the principles we are learning in this series is to memorize key Scriptures. For many, memorization is a new concept or one that has been difficult in the past. We encourage you to stretch yourself and try to memorize these four key verses. If possible, memorize these as a group and make them part of your group time. You may cut these apart and carry them in your wallet.

I have hidden your word in my heart that I might not sin against you.

Psalm 119:11 (NIV)

Session One

You alone are the LORD. You made the heavens, even the highest heavens, and all their starry host, the earth and all that is on it, the seas and all that is in them. You give life to everything, and the multitudes of heaven worship you.

Nehemiah 9:6 (NIV)

Session Two

The heavens tell the glory of God, and the skies announce what his hands have made.

Psalm 19:1 (NCV)

Session Three

By faith we understand that the universe was formed at God's command, so that what is seen was not made out of what was visible.

Hebrews 11:3 (NIV)

Session Four

He existed before everything else began, and he holds all creation together.

Colossians 1:17 (NLT)

NOTES

We value your thoughts about what you've just read.
Please share them with us. You'll find contact information
in the back of this book.

The Purpose Driven® Life
A six-session video-based study for groups or individuals

Embark on a journey of discovery with this video-based study taught by Rick Warren. In it you will discover the answer to life's most fundamental question: "What on earth am I here for?"

And here's a clue to the answer: It's not about you . . . You were created by God and for God, and until you understand that, life will never make sense. It is only in God that we discover our origin, our identity, our meaning, our purpose, our significance, and our destiny."

Whether you experience this adventure with a small group or on your own, this six-session, video-based study will change your life.

DVD Study Guide: 978-0-310-27866-5
DVD: 978-0-310-27864-1

Be sure to combine this study with your reading of the best-selling book, *The Purpose Driven® Life*, to give you or your small group the opportunity to discuss the implications and applications of living the life God created you to live.

Hardcover, Jacketed: 978-0-310-20571-5
Softcover: 978-0-310-27699-9

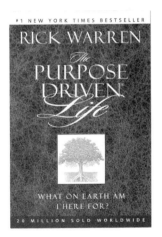

Pick up a copy today at your favorite bookstore!

Foundations: 11 Core Truths to Build Your Life On

Taught by Tom Holladay and Kay Warren

Foundations is a series of 11 four-week video studies covering the most important, foundational doctrines of the Christian faith. Study topics include:

The Bible—This study focuses on where the Bible came from, why it can be trusted, and how it can change your life.

DVD Study Guide: 978-0-310-27670-8
DVD: 978-0-310-27669-2

God—This study focuses not just on facts about God, but on how to know God himself in a more powerful and personal way.

DVD Study Guide: 978-0-310-27672-2
DVD: 978-0-310-27671-5

Jesus—As we look at what the Bible says about the person of Christ, we do so as people who are developing a lifelong relationship with Jesus.

DVD Study Guide: 978-0-310-27674-6
DVD: 978-0-310-27673-9

The Holy Spirit—This study focuses on the person, the presence, and the power of the Holy Spirit, and how you can be filled with the Holy Spirit on a daily basis.

DVD Study Guide: 978-0-310-27676-0
DVD: 978-0-310-27675-3

Creation—Each of us was personally created by a loving God. This study does not shy away from the great scientific and theological arguments that surround the creation/evolution debate. However, you will find the goal of this study is deepening your awareness of God as your Creator.

DVD Study Guide: 978-0-310-27678-4
DVD: 978-0-310-27677-7

Pick up a copy today at your favorite bookstore!

Salvation—This study focuses on God's solution to man's need for salvation, what Jesus Christ did for us on the cross, and the assurance and security of God's love and provision for eternity.

DVD Study Guide: 978-0-310-27682-1
DVD: 978-0-310-27679-1

Sanctification—This study focuses on the two natures of the Christian. We'll see the difference between grace and law, and how these two things work in our lives.

DVD Study Guide: 978-0-310-27684-5
DVD: 978-0-310-27683-8

Good and Evil—Why do bad things happen to good people? Through this study we'll see how and why God continues to allow evil to exist. The ultimate goal is to build up our faith and relationship with God as we wrestle with these difficult questions.

DVD Study Guide: 978-0-310-27687-6
DVD: 978-0-310-27686-9

The Afterlife—The Bible does not answer all the questions we have about what happens to us after we die; however, this study deals with what the Bible does tell us. This important study gives us hope and helps us move from a focus on the here and now to a focus on eternity.

DVD Study Guide: 978-0-310-27689-0
DVD: 978-0-310-27688-3

The Church—This study focuses on the birth of the church, the nature of the church, and the mission of the church.

DVD Study Guide: 978-0-310-27692-0
DVD: 978-0-310-27691-3

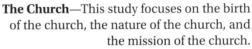
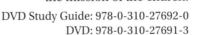

The Second Coming—This study addresses both the hope and the uncertainties surrounding the second coming of Jesus Christ.

DVD Study Guide: 978-0-310-27695-1
DVD: 978-0-310-27693-7

Pick up a copy today at your favorite bookstore!

ZONDERVAN®
.com

Celebrate Recovery, Updated Curriculum Kit

This kit will provide your church with the tools necessary to start a successful Celebrate Recovery program. *Kit includes:*

- Introductory Guide for Leaders DVD
- Leader's Guide
- 4 Participant's Guides (one of each guide)
- CD-ROM with 25 lessons
- CD-ROM with sermon transcripts
- 4-volume audio CD sermon series

Curriculum Kit: 978-0-310-26847-5

Participant's Guide 4-pack

The Celebrate Recovery Participant's Guide 4-pack is a convenient resource when you're just getting started or if you need replacement guides for your program.

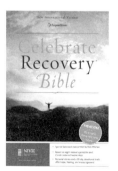

Celebrate Recovery Bible

With features based on eight principles Jesus voiced in his Sermon on the Mount, the new *Celebrate Recovery Bible* offers hope, encouragement, and empowerment for those struggling with the circumstances of their lives and the habits they are trying to control.

Hardcover 978-0-310-92849-2
Softcover 978-0-310-93810-1

Pick up a copy today at your favorite bookstore!

ZONDERVAN®
.com

Stepping Out of Denial into God's Grace

Participant's Guide 1 introduces the eight principles of recovery based on Jesus' words in the Beatitudes, and focuses on principles 1–3. Participants learn about denial, hope, sanity, and more.

Getting Right with God, Yourself, and Others

Participant's Guide 3 covers principles 5–7 based on Jesus' words in the Beatitudes. With courage and support from their fellow participants, people seeking recovery will find victory, forgiveness, and grace.

Taking an Honest and Spiritual Inventory

Participant's Guide 2 focuses on the fourth principle based on Jesus' words in the Beatitudes and builds on the Scripture, *"Happy are the pure in heart."* (Matthew 5:8) The participant will learn an invaluable principle for recovery and also take an in-depth spiritual inventory.

Growing in Christ While Helping Others

Participant's Guide 4 walks through the final steps of the eight recovery principles based on Jesus' words in the Beatitudes. In this final phase, participants learn to move forward in newfound freedom in Christ, learning how to give back to others. There's even a practical lesson called "Seven reasons we get stuck in our recoveries."

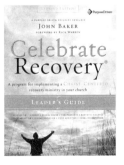

Leader's Guide

The Celebrate Recovery Leader's Guide gives you everything you need to facilitate your preparation time. Virtually walking you through every meeting, the Leader's Guide is a must-have for every leader on your Celebrate Recovery ministry team.

Pick up a copy today at your favorite bookstore!

Wide Angle:
Framing Your Worldview

Christianity is much more than a religion. It is a worldview—a way of seeing all of life and the world around you. Your worldview impacts virtually every decision you make in life: moral decisions, relational decisions, financial decisions— everything. How you see the world determines how you face the world.

In this brand new study, Rick Warren and Chuck Colson discuss such key issues as moral relativism, tolerance, terrorism, creationism vs. Darwinism, sin and suffering. They explore in depth the Christian worldview as it relates to the most important questions in life:

- Why does it matter what I believe?

- How do I know what's true?

- Where do I come from?

- Why is the world so messed up?

- Is there a solution?

- What is my purpose in life?

Rick Warren   *Chuck Colson*

This study is as deep as it is wide, addressing vitally important topics for every follower of Christ.

DVD Study Guide: 978-1-4228-0083-6
DVD: 978-1-4228-0082-9

The Way of a Worshiper

The pursuit of God is the chase of a lifetime—in fact, it's been going on since the day you were born. The question is: Have you been the hunter or the prey?

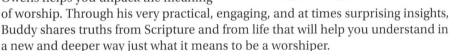

This small group study is not about music. It's not even about going to church. It's about living your life as an offering of worship to God. It's about tapping into the source of power to live the Christian life. And it's about discovering the secret to friendship with God.

In these four video sessions, Buddy Owens helps you unpack the meaning of worship. Through his very practical, engaging, and at times surprising insights, Buddy shares truths from Scripture and from life that will help you understand in a new and deeper way just what it means to be a worshiper.

God is looking for worshipers. His invitation to friendship is open and genuine. Will you take him up on his offer? Will you give yourself to him in worship? Then come walk *The Way of a Worshiper* and discover the secret to friendship with God.

DVD Study Guide: 978-1-4228-0096-6
DVD: 978-1-4228-0095-9

THE WAY *of a* WORSHIPER

Your study of this material will be greatly enhanced by reading the book, *The Way of a Worshiper: Discover the Secret to Friendship with God.*

Managing Our Finances God's Way

Did you know that there are over 2,350 verses in the Bible about money? Did you know that nearly half of Jesus' parables are about possessions? The Bible is packed with wise counsel about your financial life. In fact, Jesus had more to say about money than about heaven and hell combined.

Introducing a new video-based small group study that will inspire you to live debt free! Created by Saddleback Church and Crown Financial Ministries, learn what the Bible has to say about our finances from Rick Warren, Chip Ingram, Ron Blue, Howard Dayton, and Chuck Bentley as they address important topics like:

- God's Solution to Debt
- Saving and Investing
- Plan Your Spending
- Giving as an Act of Worship
- Enjoy What God Has Given You

Study includes:

- DVD with seven 20-minute lessons

- Workbook with seven lessons

- Resource CD with digital version of all worksheets that perform calculations automatically

- Contact information for help with answering questions

- Resources for keeping financial plans on track and making them lifelong habits

NOTE: PARTICIPANTS DO NOT SHARE PERSONAL FINANCIAL INFORMATION WITH EACH OTHER.

DVD Study Guide: 978-1-4228-0083-6
DVD: 978-1-4228-0082-9

Share Your Thoughts

With the Author: Your comments will be forwarded to the author when you send them to *zauthor@zondervan.com*.

With Zondervan: Submit your review of this book by writing to *zreview@zondervan.com*.

Free Online Resources at
www.zondervan.com/hello

 Zondervan AuthorTracker: Be notified whenever your favorite authors publish new books, go on tour, or post an update about what's happening in their lives.

 Daily Bible Verses and Devotions: Enrich your life with daily Bible verses or devotions that help you start every morning focused on God.

 Free Email Publications: Sign up for newsletters on fiction, Christian living, church ministry, parenting, and more.

 Zondervan Bible Search: Find and compare Bible passages in a variety of translations at www.zondervanbiblesearch.com.

 Other Benefits: Register yourself to receive online benefits like coupons and special offers, or to participate in research.